The Power and Potential of Natural Language Processing

Preface

Natural Language Processing (NLP) is a rapidly growing field that is revolutionizing the way we interact with technology. From voice assistants to chatbots and machine translation, NLP is making it possible for machines to understand and respond to human language.

This book is intended to provide an introduction to the fundamental concepts and techniques of NLP. It is designed for readers with a basic understanding of programming and mathematics who are interested in exploring the field of NLP. The book covers a wide range of topics, from basic text processing techniques to advanced machine learning models.

The book is organized into several sections, each covering a different aspect of NLP. The first section introduces the fundamental concepts of NLP, including tokenization, stemming, and part-of-speech tagging. The second section covers advanced text processing techniques such as named entity recognition, sentiment analysis, and topic modeling. The third section focuses on machine learning models for NLP, including classification models, sequence models, and deep learning models.

In addition to the theoretical concepts, the book also includes practical examples and case studies to demonstrate how NLP can be applied in real-world scenarios. The book also includes a section on resources for NLP, such as pre-trained models, word embeddings, lexicons, and corpora.

As with any rapidly evolving field, there are many challenges and opportunities in NLP. The book concludes with a discussion of future trends and challenges in NLP, including ethical considerations, multi-lingual NLP, and explainable AI.

We hope this book will be a valuable resource for anyone wanting to learn more about NLP and its applications. We would like to point out here that because it is such a rapidly changing field, it is possible that information in this book is outdated. The reader should be aware of this. With that said, we conclude by saying that we believe NLP has the potential to transform the way we interact with technology, and we're excited to be a part of this exciting field.

A. Scholtens

Table of Contents

Chapter 1: Introduction to Natural Language Processing

Natural Language Processing (NLP) is a subfield of artificial intelligence that focuses on enabling computers to understand, interpret, and generate human language. NLP is a multidisciplinary field that draws on techniques from computer science, linguistics, mathematics, and psychology to build systems that can analyze and generate human language data.

NLP has become increasingly important in recent years due to the explosive growth of digital data and the need to make sense of large volumes of text data. NLP is used in a wide range of applications, from virtual assistants and chatbots to sentiment analysis and machine translation.

The main tasks of NLP can be broadly categorized into the following categories:

1. Text Classification: Text classification involves categorizing text documents into predefined categories based on their content. Examples of text classification tasks include spam filtering, sentiment analysis, and topic classification.

2. Named Entity Recognition: Named Entity Recognition (NER) involves identifying entities in text, such as people, places, and organizations, and classifying them into predefined categories. NER is an important task in information extraction and text analysis.

3. Information Retrieval: Information Retrieval involves retrieving relevant documents from a collection of documents based on a user's

query. Search engines are an example of an information retrieval system.

4. Text Summarization: Text summarization involves generating a concise and coherent summary of a long document or set of documents. Text summarization is useful for quickly understanding the content of a large volume of text.

5. Machine Translation: Machine Translation involves translating text from one language to another. Machine Translation is used in various applications, such as cross-lingual information retrieval and international communication.

The importance of NLP in various fields cannot be overstated. NLP has become an essential tool in many industries, including healthcare, finance, marketing, and customer service. For example, in healthcare, NLP is used to extract clinical information from electronic medical records and to develop predictive models for disease diagnosis and treatment. In finance, NLP is used for sentiment analysis of financial news and social media to predict stock prices and market trends. In marketing, NLP is used for customer sentiment analysis to improve customer engagement and satisfaction. NLP is also used in customer service to develop chatbots and virtual assistants that can provide 24/7 support to customers.

NLP is a fascinating field that has made significant advances in recent years, enabling computers to understand, analyze, and generate human language. The potential applications of NLP are vast and range from healthcare to finance to marketing. In the following chapters, we will explore the various techniques and tools used in NLP and how they can be applied to solve real-world problems.

Chapter 2: Data Preprocessing in Natural Language Processing

Data preprocessing is an essential step in Natural Language Processing (NLP) that involves transforming raw text data into a format that can be used for analysis and modeling. Data preprocessing involves several tasks, such as cleaning and formatting text data, tokenization, stemming, stop words removal, part of speech tagging, and named entity recognition.

2.1 Cleaning and Formatting Text Data

Cleaning and formatting text data helps to improve the quality and accuracy of the text data. Text data often contains various types of noise, such as special characters, punctuation marks, and numbers, which can interfere with the analysis and modeling process. Noise elements can also make it difficult to extract meaningful information from the text data.

For example, consider the following text: "I love apples!!! They are the best :D."

If this text is not cleaned and formatted properly, it may be difficult to extract meaningful information from it. The exclamation marks and smiley face emoticon may be interpreted as noise, making it difficult to identify the sentiment of the text.

Cleaning and formatting text data involves several steps. First, unwanted characters, symbols, and numbers are removed from the text data. This can be done using regular expressions or string manipulation techniques. For example, punctuation marks, special characters, and digits can be removed using regular expressions.

Next, text data may contain multiple lines, tabs, or extra spaces, which need to be removed or replaced with a single space. This can be done using string manipulation techniques or regular expressions. For example, multiple spaces can be replaced with a single space using regular expressions.

Cleaning and formatting text data can also involve other tasks, such as converting text to lowercase or uppercase and removing HTML tags or URLs from the text data.

2.2 Tokenization and Stemming

Tokenization and stemming both help to transform unstructured text data into a structured format, which can be easily processed and analyzed.

Tokenization involves breaking down text data into individual tokens or words. This process is done by using certain rules or patterns to split the text data into individual tokens. For example, a simple way to tokenize text data is by splitting the text data using spaces. However, this approach may not be sufficient in cases where the text data contains punctuation marks, special characters, or other forms of noise.

Advanced tokenization techniques, such as using regular expressions or machine learning models, can be used to handle such cases. Tokenization is an important step because it enables the NLP algorithms to identify the underlying structure of the text data and analyze it accordingly.

Stemming, on the other hand, is a process that involves reducing words to their base form or stem. For example, the words "running," "runs," and "ran" can all be stemmed to "run." Stemming helps to reduce the dimensionality of the text data by collapsing words with the same stem into a single term. This is important because it helps to reduce the complexity of the text data and makes it easier to analyze.

There are different algorithms that can be used for stemming, such as the Porter stemming algorithm and the Snowball stemming algorithm. These algorithms work by removing common suffixes from the words to obtain their stems. However, it is important to note that stemming can sometimes result in loss of information, as different words with different meanings may be reduced to the same stem.

2.3 Stop Words Removal

Stop words are common words that are frequently used in language but do not contribute much meaning to the text data. Examples of stop words include "the," "a," "an," "and," "in," "of," and "to." These words are often used to connect other words in a sentence or to add grammatical structure to the text data.

However, in NLP, stop words can be removed from the text data to reduce noise and improve the accuracy of NLP models. This is because stop words are usually not helpful in identifying the main topic or sentiment of a text, and their presence can negatively impact the performance of NLP algorithms.

Stop words removal is typically performed after tokenization and stemming. The process involves identifying the stop words in the text data and removing them from the tokenized text. This can be done using pre-defined lists of stop words, which are commonly available in NLP libraries.

In addition to improving the accuracy of NLP models, stop words removal can also help to reduce the dimensionality of the text data. This is because removing stop words can reduce the number of unique words in the text data, making it easier to process and analyze.

However, stop words removal may not always be beneficial. In some cases, stop words may carry some meaning or context, especially in certain types of text data such as poetry or legal documents. Therefore, it is important to carefully consider the impact of stop words removal on the accuracy and quality of the NLP models being developed.

2.4 Part of Speech Tagging

Part of speech (POS) tagging is a process that involves assigning a specific grammatical category to each word in a sentence or text, such as noun, verb, adjective, adverb, pronoun, conjunction, preposition, etc. POS tagging helps to extract meaningful information from the text data and is an essential step in many NLP applications.

Assigning the correct part of speech to each word is important because it helps to determine the meaning of a sentence and the relationship between different words in the text. For example, consider the sentence "I saw the man with the telescope." Without knowing the part of speech of each word, it would be difficult to determine whether "the man" or "the telescope" was being referred to as the object of the verb "saw."

Part of speech tagging can be done using machine learning algorithms, such as Hidden Markov Models (HMMs) or Conditional Random Fields (CRFs), which use statistical patterns to predict the most likely part of speech for each word in a sentence. These algorithms are trained on large annotated datasets, which provide examples of how different words are used in different contexts.

Part of speech tagging is used in a wide range of NLP applications, such as sentiment analysis, where the sentiment of a sentence is often determined by the adjectives used in the sentence, and named entity recognition, where recognizing the part of speech of a word can help to identify whether it is a person, organization, or location.

In addition to improving the accuracy of NLP models, part of speech tagging can also help to improve the efficiency of text processing by reducing the dimensionality of the text data. This is because assigning a part of speech to each word can reduce the number of possible combinations of words and parts of speech that need to be considered in text analysis.

2.5 Named Entity Recognition

Named Entity Recognition (NER) is a task in Natural Language Processing that involves identifying and extracting named entities from unstructured text data. Named entities can be anything that has a proper name or title, such as people, places, organizations, and products.

NER is an essential task in information extraction and text analysis because it helps to identify the most important entities mentioned in a piece of text. By identifying and extracting named entities, NER can be used to answer questions such as "Who is the main character in this novel?" or "What are the names of the companies mentioned in this article?"

NER is typically performed using machine learning algorithms, which are trained on large datasets of annotated text. These algorithms use various features, such as the context in which a word appears, its part of speech, and any surrounding words or phrases, to determine whether a word is a named entity and what type of entity it is.

Once the named entities have been identified and extracted, they can be further analyzed and used in various applications. For example, in sentiment analysis, the sentiment of a text may be influenced by the named entities mentioned. In machine translation, named entities may need to be translated differently from other words to maintain their meaning.

In addition to improving the accuracy of NLP models, NER can also help to improve the efficiency of text processing by reducing the amount of text that needs to be analyzed. By identifying and extracting the most important named entities from a piece of text, NER can help to focus the analysis on the most relevant parts of the text.

2.6 Summary of the chapter

Data preprocessing is a crucial step in NLP that involves transforming raw text data into a format that can be used for analysis and modeling. Data preprocessing involves several tasks, such as cleaning and formatting text data, tokenization, stemming, stop words removal, part of speech tagging, and named entity recognition. These tasks help to extract meaningful information from the text data and reduce noise, making it easier to process and analyze. In the next chapter, we will explore various NLP techniques for text analysis, such as sentiment analysis, topic modeling, and text summarization.

Chapter 3: Text Classification

One of the essential tasks in NLP is text classification, which involves automatically assigning predefined categories or labels to text documents. In this chapter, we will discuss the definition of text classification, its importance, and various techniques used for text classification.

Definition of Text Classification

Text classification is the task of automatically assigning predefined categories or labels to a set of text documents based on their content. The categories or labels can be anything, such as topic, sentiment, genre, author, language, etc. Text classification is a supervised learning problem, where a machine learning model is trained on a labeled dataset to classify new, unseen text documents into the predefined categories.

3.1 Supervised Learning for Text Classification

Supervised learning is a popular approach for text classification because it allows the machine learning model to learn from labeled data and generalize its understanding to unseen data. In supervised learning, the labeled data is typically divided into two sets: a training set and a testing set. The training set is used to train the machine learning model, while the testing set is used to evaluate the performance of the model on unseen data.

One of the advantages of supervised learning is that it can learn complex relationships between the input features and output labels. This is important for text classification tasks, where the input features can be high-dimensional and noisy. Supervised learning algorithms can handle these challenges and identify patterns that are not immediately apparent to humans.

There are several supervised learning algorithms that can be used for text classification. Naive Bayes, Logistic Regression, and Support Vector Machine (SVM) are some of the most commonly used algorithms.

3.2 Naive Bayes Classifier

Naive Bayes assumes that the input features are conditionally independent given the category label, which means that the presence or absence of a particular word in a text document is not affected by the presence or absence of any other word in the document. This assumption simplifies the calculation of the probability of the evidence given the hypothesis, which is known as the likelihood.

The Naive Bayes classifier calculates the prior probability of each category label based on the frequency of documents in the training dataset that belong to that category. Then, it calculates the likelihood of each word in the vocabulary given each category label based on the frequency of documents in the training dataset that belong to that category and contain that word. Finally, it combines the prior probability and the likelihood to calculate the posterior probability of each category label given the input features. The category label with the highest posterior probability is chosen as the predicted label for the input document.

Despite its simplicity, Naive Bayes can achieve high accuracy in text classification tasks, especially when the input features are binary (i.e., the presence or absence of each word in the document is represented as a binary feature). However, it may not perform well when there are dependencies between the input features or when the input features have continuous values.

3.3 Logistic Regression Classifier

Logistic regression is a widely used statistical model for binary classification tasks in machine learning, including text classification. It is a probabilistic model that uses a logistic function to map the input features to the output probability of belonging to a specific category.

In text classification, the input features are typically the words or n-grams in the document, and the output labels are the predefined categories. The logistic regression model learns the weights for each input feature, which represent how important that feature is for predicting the output label.

During the training phase, the logistic regression model optimizes its parameters to minimize the difference between the predicted probability and the actual label. The optimization is typically done using gradient descent or other optimization techniques.

One of the advantages of logistic regression is its simplicity and interpretability. The model outputs a probability score between 0 and 1, which can be interpreted as the confidence level of the prediction. The weights learned by the model can also be examined to understand which features are most important for predicting the output label.

Logistic regression is a popular choice for text classification tasks because it can handle high-dimensional input features and can learn non-linear relationships between the features and the output labels. However, it may not perform well in cases where the data is highly imbalanced or when the input features are highly correlated. In such cases, other classifiers, such as Support Vector Machines (SVMs), may be more appropriate.

3.4 Support Vector Machine (SVM) Classifier

Support Vector Machine (SVM) is a powerful and widely used algorithm in text classification. SVM is a binary classifier, which means it classifies text data into two classes, i.e., positive and negative, spam and not spam, or any other relevant classes. The SVM algorithm works by finding a hyperplane that maximizes the margin between the two classes in a high-dimensional feature space. The points closest to the hyperplane are called support vectors, and they are used to define the decision boundary.

The SVM algorithm can handle both linear and nonlinear classification problems, making it suitable for a wide range of text classification tasks. In linear SVM, the hyperplane is a linear decision boundary, which separates the two classes. In contrast, in nonlinear SVM, the hyperplane can be a nonlinear decision boundary that separates the two classes in a high-dimensional feature space.

SVM has several advantages over other classification algorithms. It is known for its ability to handle high-dimensional data and large datasets. SVM can also handle data that is not linearly separable by mapping the data to a higher-dimensional feature space. Additionally, SVM is less prone to overfitting, which is a common problem in text classification, especially when the dataset is small.

The SVM algorithm has several parameters that need to be tuned to achieve optimal performance. These parameters include the kernel type, regularization parameter, and kernel coefficient. The kernel type determines the type of decision boundary used by the SVM algorithm. The regularization parameter controls the trade-off between maximizing the margin and minimizing the classification error. The kernel coefficient determines the degree of nonlinearity in the decision boundary.

3.5 Evaluation Metrics for Text Classification

Once the text classification model has been trained and tested on a labeled dataset, it is important to evaluate its performance using appropriate evaluation metrics. Accuracy, precision, recall, and F1-score are all metrics used to evaluate the performance of a text classification model. However, they each measure different aspects of the model's performance.

Accuracy is the most straightforward metric and is simply the percentage of correctly classified documents. While accuracy can be useful, it can be misleading when the dataset is imbalanced, meaning that one category has significantly more examples than others. In such cases, a model can achieve high accuracy by simply predicting the majority class for every example.

Precision measures the ratio of true positives to the total number of documents predicted as positive. It is a measure of how many of the predicted positive documents are actually positive. High precision indicates that the model is making few false positive errors.

Recall measures the ratio of true positives to the total number of positive documents. It is a measure of how many of the positive documents are correctly identified by the model. High recall indicates that the model is making few false negative errors.

F1-score is the harmonic mean of precision and recall. It balances both metrics and is a good overall measure of a model's performance.

In addition to these metrics, it is also important to consider other factors such as the size and quality of the dataset, the choice of features and algorithms, and the computational resources available. Evaluating the performance of a text classification model can be an iterative process, where different parameters and configurations are tried and tested until a satisfactory level of performance is achieved.

3.6 Summary of the chapter

Text classification is an essential task in NLP that involves automatically assigning predefined categories or labels to text documents. Supervised learning is the most commonly used approach for text classification, and various classifiers such as Naive Bayes, Logistic Regression, and SVM are used for this purpose. Finally, evaluation metrics such as accuracy, precision, recall, and F1-score are used to evaluate the performance of text classification models.

Chapter 4: Sentiment Analysis

Sentiment analysis, also known as opinion mining, is the process of identifying, extracting, and quantifying subjective information from text data. It involves analyzing the emotional tone, attitude, and opinion expressed in the text data, such as reviews, feedback, social media posts, and news articles. Sentiment analysis has become increasingly important in recent years, as organizations use it to gain insights into customer feedback, monitor brand reputation, and make data-driven decisions.

Definition of Sentiment Analysis

Sentiment analysis is the process of using natural language processing, computational linguistics, and machine learning techniques to automatically identify, extract, and quantify the emotional tone, attitude, and opinion expressed in text data. The emotional tone can be positive, negative, or neutral, and the attitude can be subjective or objective.

Different Approaches to Sentiment Analysis

There are three main approaches to sentiment analysis: lexicon-based, machine learning-based, and deep learning-based.

4.2 Lexicon-Based Sentiment Analysis

Lexicon-based sentiment analysis is a rule-based approach that relies on the knowledge captured in pre-built dictionaries or lexicons. These lexicons are collections of words and phrases that are manually annotated with their corresponding sentiment scores. Typically, a positive sentiment score indicates a positive sentiment or emotion, while a negative score indicates a negative sentiment or emotion.

The lexicon-based sentiment analysis approach can be divided into two categories: dictionary-based and corpus-based. In dictionary-based approaches, the sentiment scores of the words in the text are looked up in the pre-built lexicon, and the overall sentiment score of the text is computed by aggregating the scores of the individual words. In contrast, corpus-based approaches use statistical methods to compute the sentiment score of the text based on the frequency of the words with positive or negative sentiment in a corpus of training data.

One of the most popular lexicons used in sentiment analysis is the AFINN lexicon, which contains over 2,400 English words with a sentiment score ranging from -5 to 5. The sentiment score of a text is computed by summing the scores of the individual words in the text. Another popular lexicon is the SentiWordNet, which is a lexical resource that assigns sentiment scores to synsets (i.e., sets of synonyms) in WordNet, a lexical database for English.

Lexicon-based sentiment analysis has several advantages. It is simple to implement, does not require large amounts of labeled data, and is computationally efficient. However, it has some limitations. It may not perform well in cases where the sentiment of the text is not captured by the words in the lexicon or when the text contains sarcasm, irony, or other forms of figurative language. Additionally, it may not perform well in multilingual settings, as it requires lexicons for each language.

4.3 Machine Learning-Based Sentiment Analysis

Machine learning-based sentiment analysis typically involves a variety of pre-processing techniques such as tokenization, stop-word removal, and stemming to prepare the text data for analysis. Once the text data is preprocessed, the next step is to extract relevant features from the text data. The most commonly used features in machine learning-based sentiment analysis are the bag-of-words and n-grams.

In the bag-of-words approach, a text document is represented as a bag of words, where the frequency of each word in the document is used as a feature. This approach ignores the order of the words in the text data but takes into account the frequency of the words, which can provide useful information about the sentiment of the text.

In the n-gram approach, a text document is represented as a sequence of n consecutive words, where n is a hyperparameter that can be set to any integer value. The n-gram approach takes into account the order of the words in the text data, which can provide more context about the sentiment of the text.

Once the features are extracted, a supervised learning model such as Naive Bayes, Logistic Regression, or Support Vector Machine (SVM) can be trained on a labeled dataset of text data to predict the sentiment of new, unseen text data. The performance of the model can be evaluated using evaluation metrics such as accuracy, precision, recall, and F1-score.

Machine learning-based sentiment analysis has been shown to be effective in many applications, such as analyzing customer reviews, social media sentiment, and political sentiment. However, it requires a large amount of labeled data for training and can be computationally expensive, especially when dealing with large volumes of text data.

To overcome these limitations, deep learning-based sentiment analysis has emerged as a promising approach in recent years.

4.4 Deep Learning-Based Sentiment Analysis

One of the popular deep learning architectures used in sentiment analysis is Convolutional Neural Networks (CNNs), which can capture local patterns and relationships between adjacent words in the text. CNNs consist of multiple convolutional layers that apply a set of learnable filters to the input text data to generate a feature map, followed by pooling layers that downsample the feature map to retain the most important features. Finally, the output of the pooling layers is passed through one or more fully connected layers to predict the sentiment label.

Another popular deep learning architecture used in sentiment analysis is Recurrent Neural Networks (RNNs), which can capture the temporal dependencies and long-term relationships between words in the text. RNNs process the input text data sequentially, one word at a time, and maintain a hidden state that encodes the information from previous words in the text. The output of the RNN is then passed through one or more fully connected layers to predict the sentiment label.

Transformer models are another powerful deep learning architecture used in sentiment analysis, which use self-attention mechanisms to capture the global dependencies and long-term relationships between words in the text. Transformer models consist of multiple encoder layers that apply self-attention mechanisms to the input text data to generate a contextualized representation of each word in the text. Finally, the output of the encoder layers is passed through one or more fully connected layers to predict the sentiment label.

Deep learning-based sentiment analysis has shown significant improvement over traditional machine learning and lexicon-based approaches in terms of accuracy and robustness. However, they require a large amount of labeled data and computational resources for training and inference.

4.5 Evaluation Metrics for Sentiment Analysis

Sentiment analysis evaluation metrics: Once the sentiment analysis model has been trained and tested on a labeled data set, it is important to evaluate its performance using the appropriate evaluation metrics, such as accuracy, precision, recall, and F1 score.

4.6 Summary of the chapter

Sentiment analysis is a critical component of natural language processing and is used in various applications, such as social media monitoring, customer feedback analysis, and brand reputation management. It involves different approaches, including lexicon-based, machine learning-based, and deep learning-based sentiment analysis. Each approach has its own advantages and limitations, and the choice of approach depends on the specific application and available data. It is important to evaluate the performance of the sentiment analysis model using appropriate evaluation metrics to ensure its effectiveness and accuracy.

Chapter 5: Text Generation

Text generation is the process of creating new text based on a given input or context. In this chapter, we will explore some of the popular approaches to text generation, including rule-based text generation, statistical language models, recurrent neural networks (RNNs), and sequence-to-sequence models.

5.1 Rule-Based Text Generation

Rule-based text generation is a traditional method used to generate natural language text using a set of predefined rules or templates. In this approach, the text generation process follows a series of rules and instructions to create new text. The rules can be based on syntax, grammar, or other linguistic rules, and they are designed to generate text that follows a specific format or structure. Rule-based text generation is often used for generating simple text, such as email responses or chatbot messages.

One of the advantages of rule-based text generation is that it can be straightforward to implement and does not require large amounts of training data. It is also highly interpretable, as the rules can be easily inspected and modified by humans. However, the limitations of rule-based text generation are that it can only generate text based on the predefined rules and cannot adapt to new contexts or generate complex text.

For example, a rule-based text generator for a customer service chatbot may have predefined rules for responding to frequently asked questions, such as

"What is your return policy?" or "What are your business hours?" The generator would follow a set of rules to generate appropriate responses to these questions, such as providing the return policy information or business hours. However, if a customer asks a question that is not covered by the predefined rules, the generator may not be able to provide a satisfactory response.

5.2 Statistical Language

To generate text using a statistical language model, the model first needs to be trained on a large corpus of text data. During training, the model learns the statistical patterns and relationships between words in the text data. The n-gram model is trained by counting the occurrences of n-word sequences in the training corpus and then calculating the probability of the next word given the previous n-1 words.

Once the statistical language model is trained, it can be used to generate new text by selecting the most probable word for each position in the sequence, based on the probability distribution learned during training. This is known as the maximum likelihood estimation approach.

While statistical language models are useful for generating simple text, they have some limitations. One of the limitations is that they cannot generate long-term dependencies between words in the text, as they only consider a fixed number of previous words. Additionally, they can generate text that is grammatically correct but semantically meaningless.

To address these limitations, more sophisticated models such as Recurrent Neural Networks (RNNs) and sequence-to-sequence models have been developed.

5.3 Recurrent Neural Networks (RNNs)

RNNs are powerful models for text generation because they can capture long-term dependencies between words in a sentence, unlike traditional feedforward neural networks that treat each input as independent. RNNs have a feedback loop that allows them to use the previous output as input to the next step in the sequence, which enables the network to remember previous inputs and use that information to generate the next output.

There are several types of RNN architectures used for text generation, including simple RNNs, LSTM (Long Short-Term Memory) networks, and GRU (Gated Recurrent Unit) networks.

5.3.1 Long Short-Term Memory (LSTM)

LSTM (Long Short-Term Memory) networks are a type of RNN that are designed to address the vanishing gradient problem, which can occur when training traditional RNNs on long sequences of data. The vanishing gradient problem refers to the issue where the gradients used to update the weights during backpropagation become very small as they propagate backwards through the network, making it difficult for the network to learn long-term dependencies.

LSTM networks use a more complex architecture than traditional RNNs, with special memory cells that are capable of retaining information over longer periods of time. The key idea behind the LSTM architecture is to have a memory cell that can selectively forget or retain information at each time step, based on the input and the previous state of the cell.

An LSTM cell has three gates: the input gate, the forget gate, and the output gate. The input gate controls how much of the new input information is added to the cell state, while the forget gate controls how much of the previous cell state is retained. The output gate controls how much of the cell state is output to the next layer of the network.

The equations for an LSTM cell are:

$$
\begin{aligned}
f_t &= \sigma(W_f x_t + U_f h_{t-1} + b_f) \\
i_t &= \sigma(W_i x_t + U_i h_{t-1} + b_i) \\
o_t &= \sigma(W_o x_t + U_o h_{t-1} + b_o) \\
c_t &= f_t \odot c_{t-1} + i_t \odot \tanh(W_c x_t + U_c h_{t-1} + b_c) \\
h_t &= o_t \odot \tanh(c_t)
\end{aligned}
$$

where:

- x_t is the input at time step t

- h_{t-1} is the output of the previous LSTM cell
- f_t, i_t, and o_t are the forget, input, and output gates, respectively
- c_t is the cell state at time step t

- h_t is the output of the current LSTM cell
- σ is the sigmoid activation function
- $\odot$ is the element-wise multiplication
- W and U are weight matrices, and b is a bias vector

LSTM networks have been used for a wide range of applications, including language modeling, machine translation, speech recognition, and text generation.

Here's an example of how an LSTM network can help maintain context over a longer sequence:

Let's say we want to generate text for a story that involves a character named John. If we were using a traditional RNN, the network would take in the first few words of the story (e.g. "John went to the store"), and then try to generate the next word based on the current input and the previous hidden state. However, as the story progresses and we introduce new characters, settings, and events, the network may have trouble remembering important details about John or other parts of the story.

With an LSTM network, the cell state acts as a sort of "memory" that can store information about John and other relevant details from earlier in the story. The network can selectively add or remove information from the cell state as needed, using input and forget gates to control the flow of information. This allows the network to maintain context over a longer sequence and generate more coherent and meaningful text.

Simple RNNs suffer from the vanishing gradient problem, which can make it difficult for them to remember information from earlier in the sequence.

5.3.2 GRU networks

Gated Recurrent Units (GRUs) are a type of recurrent neural network that is similar to LSTM networks. GRUs were introduced by Cho et al. in 2014 and have been shown to be effective in various natural language processing tasks, including text generation, machine translation, and sentiment analysis.

GRUs are simpler than LSTMs and have fewer parameters, making them faster to train and less prone to overfitting. The key difference between GRUs and LSTMs is the number of gates they use to control the flow of information in the network. While LSTMs have three gates (input gate, forget gate, and output gate), GRUs have two gates (reset gate and update gate).

The reset gate in a GRU network is used to determine how much of the previous hidden state should be forgotten, while the update gate is used to determine how much of the current input should be added to the new hidden state. GRUs also use a single candidate hidden state that combines the previous hidden state and the current input.

The equations for a GRU are as follows:

- Reset gate: $r_t = sigmoid(W_r * x_t + U_r * h_{\{t-1\}} + b_r)$
- Update gate: $z_t = sigmoid(W_z * x_t + U_z * h_{\{t-1\}} + b_z)$
- Candidate hidden state: $\tilde{h}t = tanh(W_h * x_t + U_h * (r_t * h{t-1}) + b_h)$
- New hidden state: $h_t = (1 - z_t) * h_{\{t-1\}} + z_t * \tilde{h}_t$

Where x_t is the input at time step t, h_t is the hidden state at time step t, r_t is the reset gate at time step t, z_t is the update gate at time step t, and $\tilde{h}_t$ is the candidate hidden state at time step t.

here's an example of how a GRU network can be used for text generation:

Let's say we have a sentence "The cat sat on the mat" and we want to generate a new sentence that follows a similar structure. We can use a GRU network to generate the new sentence by predicting each word based on the previous words.

First, we encode the input sentence into a sequence of word embeddings. The word embeddings are fed into the GRU network, which learns to predict the next word based on the previous words. The GRU network has a hidden state that stores information from the previous time steps and uses it to make predictions for the next time step.

For example, let's say the GRU network has been trained on a corpus of text and has learned that after the phrase "The cat sat on", the next word is often "the mat". The network can use this knowledge to generate a new sentence by predicting the next word based on the previous words.

During the generation process, the network generates a probability distribution over the possible next words based on the hidden state and the previous word. The word with the highest probability is selected as the next word, and the process is repeated until the desired length of the sentence is reached.

The GRU network can also be conditioned on some additional information, such as the desired sentiment or topic of the generated text, by adding extra input to the network or adjusting the loss function during training.

GRUs have shown to perform well on various natural language processing tasks, including sentiment analysis, text generation, and machine translation. However, the choice of the type of RNN to use (LSTM or GRU) ultimately depends on the specific task and the available data.

5.3.3 Sequence-to-Sequence

In sequence-to-sequence modeling, the RNN is typically divided into two parts: an encoder and a decoder. The encoder takes the input sequence and compresses it into a fixed-length vector representation called a "context vector". The decoder then takes the context vector and generates the output sequence word by word.

One of the popular models used for sequence-to-sequence text generation is the Encoder-Decoder model. In this model, the encoder and decoder are both RNNs, and the output of the encoder RNN is used as the initial hidden state of the decoder RNN. The decoder generates the output sequence word by word, using the context vector and the previously generated words as input.

Another popular model used for sequence-to-sequence text generation is the Transformer model. The Transformer model uses a self-attention mechanism to capture the dependencies between the input and output sequences, which allows it to generate more accurate and fluent text. The Transformer model has been used successfully in various text generation tasks such as machine translation, summarization, and question answering.

5.4 Text Generation Challenges

Text generation using RNNs has several challenges, including the generation of coherent and meaningful text, avoiding repetition or generating gibberish. Researchers have proposed several evaluation metrics to measure the quality of generated text, including perplexity, BLEU (bilingual evaluation understudy), and ROUGE (recall-oriented understudy for gisting evaluation). These metrics are used to evaluate the similarity between the generated text and the original text, as well as the fluency and coherence of the generated text.

5.4.1 BLEU

BLEU (bilingual evaluation understudy) is a metric commonly used to evaluate the quality of machine-generated text. It was initially designed for evaluating the quality of machine translation systems, but it is now widely used in other natural language processing tasks, including text generation. BLEU measures the similarity between the machine-generated text and the reference text by comparing the n-gram overlap between them. It calculates a score between 0 and 1, where 1 represents perfect similarity. Although BLEU has some limitations and does not always correlate well with human judgments, it remains a widely used metric for evaluating the quality of machine-generated text.

5.4.2 ROGUE

ROUGE (Recall-Oriented Understudy for Gisting Evaluation) is another commonly used evaluation metric for text generation. It measures the similarity between the generated text and the reference text based on the overlapping of n-grams (contiguous sequences of words) between the two texts. ROUGE has been widely used for evaluating the quality of machine-generated summaries and is often reported alongside BLEU scores. ROUGE scores range from 0 to 1, with higher scores indicating better text generation performance.

5.4.3 Human Evaluation

Human evaluation is a subjective approach to evaluate the quality of generated text. In this approach, human evaluators are asked to rate the quality of generated text based on various aspects such as fluency, coherence, relevance, and overall quality. Human evaluation can provide valuable insights into the quality of generated text, as it takes into account the nuances and complexities of human language that are difficult to quantify using automatic metrics. However, human evaluation can be time-consuming and expensive, and the results may be subject to biases and individual preferences of the evaluators. Therefore, it is often used in combination with automatic evaluation metrics to provide a more comprehensive evaluation of generated text.

5.5 Summary of the chapter

Text generation is a fascinating area of natural language processing that has seen significant progress in recent years. The approaches discussed in this chapter, including rule-based text generation, statistical language models, recurrent neural networks (RNNs), and sequence-to-sequence models, have shown remarkable success in generating new text. However, the evaluation of text generation is still an open research problem, and researchers are actively working on developing better evaluation metrics.

Chapter 6: Topic Modeling

Topic modeling is a technique used to extract latent topics from a collection of text documents. It is a form of unsupervised learning that identifies the hidden semantic structure in a corpus of text data. Topic modeling can be used for various applications such as text classification, information retrieval, and recommendation systems.

6.1 Latent Dirichlet Allocation (LDA)

Latent Dirichlet Allocation (LDA) is a popular topic modeling algorithm that was introduced in 2003 by David Blei, Andrew Ng, and Michael Jordan. LDA assumes that each document is a mixture of topics, and each topic is a mixture of words. The algorithm assigns a probability distribution to each word in the corpus, indicating its likelihood of belonging to each topic. LDA works by iteratively adjusting the topic probabilities until the model converges.

To better understand how LDA works, let's consider an example. Suppose we have a corpus of 100 articles, and we want to identify the topics that are present in the corpus. We can use LDA to model the topics and their associated words as probability distributions.

First, we need to choose the number of topics we want to identify. Let's say we choose 5 topics. Next, LDA will randomly assign each word in the corpus to one of the 5 topics. For example, the word "data" might be initially assigned to the "statistics" topic, and the word "network" might be initially assigned to the "computer science" topic.

In the next step, LDA will iterate through each word in the corpus and adjust the probabilities of the topics to which the word is assigned. For example, if the word "data" appears frequently in the same document as the words "statistics" and "analysis," LDA will increase the probability of the "statistics" topic and the "data analysis" topic for that word.

After several iterations, LDA will converge, and we will have a probability distribution for each topic that indicates the likelihood of each word belonging to that topic. We can then interpret the topics based on the most likely words in each topic.

LDA has been used in various applications, such as text classification, document clustering, and content-based recommendation systems. It has become one of the most widely used topic modeling algorithms due to its simplicity and effectiveness.

6.2 Non-negative Matrix Factorization (NMF)

Non-negative Matrix Factorization (NMF) is a matrix factorization technique that decomposes a non-negative matrix into two non-negative matrices of lower rank. In the context of topic modeling, the non-negative matrix represents the term-document matrix, where each row represents a document, each column represents a term, and the elements represent the frequency of each term in each document. NMF factorizes this matrix into two non-negative matrices, W and H, where W represents the topics and H represents the document-topic distribution.

NMF is based on the idea that each document is a linear combination of a small number of topics, and each topic is a distribution over terms. The algorithm iteratively updates the values of W and H until the approximation error between the original matrix and the factorization is minimized. Unlike LDA, NMF imposes a sparsity constraint on the topic matrix, making it more interpretable. This means that the elements in the topic matrix are mostly zero, which indicates that a topic only has a few highly relevant terms.

One advantage of NMF over LDA is that it can identify patterns in the data that may not be easily recognizable using LDA. NMF has been used in various applications such as text mining, image processing, and bioinformatics. However, like LDA, the performance of NMF highly depends on the quality of the input data and the choice of hyperparameters. Therefore, it is essential to evaluate the performance of the topic models generated by NMF using appropriate evaluation metrics.

6.3 Hierarchical Dirichlet Process (HDP)

Hierarchical Dirichlet Process (HDP) is an extension of LDA that is based on the Bayesian nonparametric approach. HDP is designed to allow for an unbounded number of topics, which makes it more flexible than LDA. HDP is a generative probabilistic model that assumes that each document is generated from a mixture of topics, and each topic is a distribution over words. HDP can automatically infer the number of topics in the corpus, which makes it more convenient to use than LDA.

HDP is based on the Dirichlet Process, which is a stochastic process that generates a distribution over distributions. In HDP, the Dirichlet Process is used to generate a distribution over topics. Each topic is then generated from a Dirichlet distribution, which in turn is generated from the Dirichlet Process. This hierarchical structure allows for an infinite number of topics, as new topics can be generated from the Dirichlet Process as needed.

One of the advantages of HDP over LDA is that it can discover the number of topics in the corpus automatically, without the need for manual tuning of the hyperparameters. This is achieved through a technique called "hierarchical clustering," which groups similar topics together and allows the model to learn the appropriate number of topics.

HDP has been used in a variety of applications, including text analysis, image analysis, and time series analysis. It has been shown to outperform LDA in some cases, particularly when dealing with large, complex datasets with many topics. However, HDP is computationally more expensive than LDA, and may not be suitable for all applications.

6.4 Evaluation metrics for topic modeling

Evaluation metrics for topic modeling include coherence, perplexity, and topic diversity.

6.4.1 Coherence

Coherence is a popular evaluation metric for topic models that measures the interpretability and quality of the topics generated by the model. It is based on the idea that a good topic model should produce topics that are coherent, meaning that the words within a topic are semantically related and provide a clear interpretation of the topic. Coherence can be calculated in different ways, but the most common approach is to use the coherence score, which is a measure of the degree of semantic similarity between the top words in each topic.

There are several coherence measures that have been proposed in the literature, such as C_V, C_P, UMass, and NPMI. These measures use different techniques to assess the coherence of topics, but they all rely on computing the similarity between the top words in each topic. The coherence score can range from 0 to 1, with higher scores indicating more coherent topics.

Coherence can be used to compare different topic models or to evaluate the performance of a single model over time. It is important to note that coherence is not a perfect metric, and it has its limitations. For example, coherence does not take into account the diversity of topics, and it may not capture the full range of semantic relationships between words. Nonetheless, coherence remains a useful tool for evaluating the interpretability and quality of topic models.

6.4.2 Perplexity

Perplexity is another commonly used evaluation metric for topic modeling. It is a measure of how well a language model predicts a sample of new text. In topic modeling, perplexity is used to evaluate how well the model predicts the words in a held-out test set. Specifically, the perplexity score measures how well the model can predict the probability of observing a given word, given the context of the other words in the same document.

A lower perplexity score indicates that the model is better at predicting the test set and, therefore, that the topic model is better at capturing the underlying structure of the corpus. However, it is important to note that perplexity is not a perfect metric, as it can be influenced by factors such as the size of the corpus, the number of topics, and the quality of the test set. Therefore, it is important to use perplexity in combination with other evaluation metrics to get a more complete picture of the topic model's performance.

6.4.3 Topic diversity

Topic diversity is a measure of how distinct and different the identified topics are from each other. A topic model with high topic diversity will generate topics that cover a wide range of themes and ideas, while a model with low topic diversity may generate topics that overlap or are too similar to each other.

There are several metrics used to measure topic diversity, including:

1. Exclusive KL Divergence: This measures the difference between the word distributions of different topics. A higher value indicates more distinct topics.

2. Mean Pairwise Cosine Similarity: This measures the average cosine similarity between the word distributions of different topics. A lower value indicates more distinct topics.

3. Topic Distance: This measures the distance between the centroids of different topics in a multi-dimensional topic space. A higher value indicates more distinct topics.

4. Normalized Pointwise Mutual Information (NPMI): This measures the degree of co-occurrence of words within a topic. A higher value indicates a more diverse topic, with words that are less likely to appear together in the same document.

6.5 Summary of the chapter

Overall, measuring topic diversity is important to ensure that a topic model captures a wide range of themes and ideas present in the corpus. A model with high topic diversity is more likely to be useful for downstream tasks such as information retrieval and recommendation systems.

Chapter 7: Information Retrieval

Introduction Information retrieval (IR) is the process of retrieving relevant information from a large collection of documents. It involves various techniques and models to efficiently retrieve the relevant information. The primary goal of IR is to minimize the time and effort required to find the relevant information.

7.1 Boolean Retrieval Model

The Boolean retrieval model is a popular model in information retrieval because of its simplicity and speed. The model is based on the Boolean logic operators that can be used to combine terms in a query. The Boolean operators are defined as follows:

- AND: retrieves documents that contain all the terms in the query.

- OR: retrieves documents that contain at least one of the terms in the query.

- NOT: retrieves documents that do not contain the specified term(s).

For example, consider a collection of documents that includes news articles about sports, politics, and entertainment. A user searching for articles related to "sports AND politics" would receive only documents that contain both "sports" and "politics." Alternatively, a user searching for articles related to "sports OR politics" would receive documents that include either "sports" or "politics" or both.

One of the strengths of the Boolean retrieval model is that it is easy to use and understand. Users can create complex queries using simple Boolean operators, which can help them find the exact information they need. However, the model has several limitations. One of the biggest drawbacks of the Boolean retrieval model is that it produces a binary output, which means that documents are either retrieved or not retrieved, without any ranking of the retrieved documents based on relevance. This can be a problem when dealing with large collections of documents, where it is often necessary to rank the retrieved documents based on their relevance. Additionally, the Boolean model assumes that all query terms are equally important, which may not be the case in practice.

7.2 Vector Space Model

The vector space model (VSM) is a popular information retrieval model that represents documents and queries as vectors in a high-dimensional space. In the VSM, each document is represented as a vector of terms in the collection and each query is represented as a vector of terms in the query. The basic idea behind the VSM is that documents and queries that are similar in terms of their content should be located closer together in the vector space than documents and queries that are dissimilar.

To construct the vector representation of documents and queries, the VSM typically uses the term frequency-inverse document frequency (TF-IDF) weighting scheme. This scheme assigns a weight to each term in a document that reflects the importance of the term in the document and the collection.

The weight of a term in a document is proportional to its frequency in the document, while the weight of a term in the collection is inversely proportional to its frequency in the collection.

Once the vector representation of documents and queries is constructed, the VSM computes the cosine similarity between the query vector and each document vector in the collection. The cosine similarity measures the cosine of the angle between the query vector and the document vector, and it ranges from -1 to 1. A cosine similarity of 1 indicates that the query and document vectors are identical, while a cosine similarity of -1 indicates that they are completely dissimilar.

The VSM is simple and efficient, and it can handle large collections of documents. However, it has some limitations. One of the main limitations is that it does not take into account the semantic meaning of the terms in the collection. This means that documents and queries that are semantically related may not be located close together in the vector space. To overcome this limitation, more advanced models, such as the probabilistic retrieval model and the deep learning-based models, have been developed.

7.3 Probabilistic Retrieval Model

The probabilistic retrieval model is based on the assumption that a document is relevant to a query if it is similar to the query in terms of its content. This model computes the probability of relevance of a document to a query. The probability of relevance is calculated based on the probability of generating the query from the document. The goal of the probabilistic retrieval model is to find the most probable set of documents that are relevant to the given query.

The key idea behind the probabilistic retrieval model is to represent a query as a set of terms and a document as a probability distribution over the terms. The relevance of a document to a query is determined by the degree of overlap between the query and document probability distributions. This overlap is computed using the cosine similarity measure.

One of the most popular probabilistic retrieval models is the Okapi BM25 model. This model computes the relevance score of a document to a query based on the frequency of the query terms in the document and the length of the document. The Okapi BM25 model takes into account the importance of rare terms and the effect of document length on the relevance score.

Another popular probabilistic retrieval model is the language model approach, which represents a document as a language model that generates the terms in the document. The probability of generating the query from the language model is used to compute the relevance score of the document to the query. The language model approach is effective in handling long queries and noisy documents.

The probabilistic retrieval model is widely used in modern IR systems, including search engines, document retrieval systems, and question answering systems. The effectiveness of the probabilistic retrieval model is evaluated using various evaluation metrics, such as precision, recall, F-measure, and mean average precision.

7.4 Evaluation Metrics for Information Retrieval

Evaluation metrics are used to measure the effectiveness of an IR system. The primary goal of these metrics is to assess the quality of the retrieved documents. The commonly used evaluation metrics for IR include precision, recall, F1-score, Mean Average Precision (MAP), and Normalized Discounted Cumulative Gain (NDCG).

7.4.1 Precision

Precision is an evaluation metric used in IR to measure the proportion of retrieved documents that are relevant to the query. In other words, precision measures the accuracy of the system in returning relevant documents. Precision is calculated as the ratio of the number of relevant documents retrieved to the total number of documents retrieved. It is often expressed as a percentage.

For example, if a search engine returns 20 documents in response to a query, and only 10 of them are relevant, the precision of the system is 50%. A higher precision value indicates that the system retrieves a larger proportion of relevant documents. However, a high precision value does not necessarily mean that all the relevant documents have been retrieved. Therefore, precision is often used in conjunction with recall to evaluate the performance of an IR system.

7.4.2 Recall

Recall is an evaluation metric that measures the ability of an IR system to retrieve all relevant documents for a given query. It is the ratio of the number of relevant documents retrieved by the system to the total number of relevant documents in the collection. In other words, recall measures how well the system is able to recall all relevant documents in the collection for a given query. A high recall value indicates that the system is able to retrieve most of the relevant documents, while a low recall value indicates that the system is missing relevant documents. The recall value ranges between 0 and 1, with 1 indicating perfect recall. The recall value can be calculated using the following formula:

Recall = Number of relevant documents retrieved / Total number of relevant documents in the collection.

7.4.3 F1-score

The F1-score is a commonly used evaluation metric in IR that combines the precision and recall scores into a single score. It is calculated as the harmonic mean of precision and recall. The F1-score provides a more balanced measure of performance than precision or recall alone, as it takes into account both the number of relevant documents retrieved (recall) and the proportion of retrieved documents that are relevant (precision). A higher F1-score indicates better overall performance in retrieving relevant documents.

The formula for F1-score is as follows:

F1-score = 2 * (precision * recall) / (precision + recall)

where precision is the number of relevant documents retrieved divided by the total number of documents retrieved, and recall is the number of relevant documents retrieved divided by the total number of relevant documents in the collection.

7.4.4 MAP

Mean Average Precision (MAP) is a widely used evaluation metric for IR that measures the average precision over a set of queries. MAP is commonly used in information retrieval tasks such as document retrieval and question answering. MAP computes the average precision for each query, and then takes the mean of these average precision scores. It is a useful metric because it takes into account the rank order of the retrieved documents, rather than just whether or not a relevant document was retrieved. A higher MAP score indicates better performance, where a perfect score is 1.0. However, the MAP score can be sensitive to the number of relevant documents for each query, and the order of the retrieved documents.

7.4.5 NDCG

Normalized Discounted Cumulative Gain (NDCG) is an evaluation metric used in IR to measure the quality of ranked retrieval results. NDCG is particularly useful when evaluating systems that provide ranked lists of documents in response to a query. NDCG measures the effectiveness of the ranking by comparing the list of documents returned by the system to a set of relevant documents for that query.

NDCG is calculated by comparing the ranked list of documents returned by the system to a graded relevance judgment for each document. The graded relevance judgment assigns a score to each document in the collection based on its relevance to the query. The relevance score can be binary (relevant or non-relevant), ordinal (e.g., low, medium, high), or continuous (e.g., relevance score from 0 to 1).

NDCG measures the degree to which the system ranks the relevant documents higher than the non-relevant ones. It takes into account both the relevance of the documents and their rank in the list. The NDCG score ranges from 0 to 1, with 1 indicating perfect ranking and 0 indicating the worst possible ranking.

NDCG is often used in conjunction with MAP to evaluate the effectiveness of IR systems. While MAP focuses on the average precision of the entire list of documents, NDCG focuses on the position of the relevant documents in the list. By using both MAP and NDCG, researchers can get a more complete picture of the effectiveness of an IR system.

7.5 Summary of the chapter

Information retrieval is an essential process in modern society, where there is an enormous amount of digital data available. The Boolean retrieval model, vector space model, and probabilistic retrieval model are the commonly used models for IR. Evaluation metrics such as precision, recall, F1-score, MAP, and NDCG are used to measure the effectiveness of the IR system. The IR field is continuously evolving with new techniques and models being developed to handle the increasing volume of digital data.

Chapter 8: Named Entity Recognition

Named Entity Recognition (NER) is the process of identifying and classifying named entities in text into predefined categories such as person names, organizations, locations, and more. It is an essential component of many natural language processing (NLP) applications such as information retrieval, question answering, machine translation, and more.

There are several techniques for performing NER. One approach is rule-based NER, where handcrafted rules are used to identify entities based on patterns, regular expressions, and dictionaries. This approach is often time-consuming and requires significant effort from domain experts. Another approach is statistical NER, where machine learning models are trained on labeled data to recognize named entities. This approach involves feature engineering, model selection, and hyperparameter tuning. Deep learning-based NER, which uses neural networks, has recently gained popularity due to its ability to learn features automatically and achieve state-of-the-art performance.

Evaluation metrics are used to assess the performance of NER systems. Commonly used metrics for NER include precision, recall, and F1-score. Precision is the ratio of correctly identified named entities to the total number of entities identified by the system. Recall is the ratio of correctly identified named entities to the total number of entities that should have been identified by the system. F1-score is the harmonic mean of precision and recall, which balances both metrics.

Another evaluation metric used for NER is the confusion matrix, which shows the number of true positives, false positives, true negatives, and false negatives. From the confusion matrix, other metrics such as accuracy, specificity, and sensitivity can be computed. Accuracy measures the overall correctness of the system, while specificity and sensitivity measure the ability of the system to correctly identify negative and positive examples, respectively.

8.1 Summary of the chapter

In conclusion, NER is a crucial component of many NLP applications, and there are various techniques available for performing NER, including rule-based, statistical, and deep learning-based methods. Evaluation metrics such as precision, recall, and F1-score are commonly used to assess the performance of NER systems. It is essential to choose the appropriate evaluation metrics and techniques for NER depending on the specific task and domain.

Chapter 9: Text Summarization

Introduction:

Text summarization is the process of reducing a large text document to a shorter version while retaining important information. Text summarization is an important task in natural language processing and has various applications, such as news article summarization, document summarization, and email summarization. There are two main approaches to text summarization: extractive and abstractive summarization.

9. 1 Extractive Summarization

Extractive summarization is a technique of text summarization that aims to generate a summary by selecting important sentences or phrases from the original text. This approach involves extracting the most relevant and salient information from the document and combining them into a shorter version that captures the essence of the original text.

The main advantage of extractive summarization is that it can be relatively straightforward to implement and does not require the generation of new sentences or the rephrasing of the original content. Additionally, the extracted summary sentences are usually more coherent and grammatically correct as they are directly taken from the source text.

There are several techniques used in extractive summarization, including:

1. Ranking-based: This approach involves ranking the sentences based on their importance and selecting the top-ranked sentences to form the summary. The importance of a sentence can be determined by

various features, such as the frequency of the keywords, the length of the sentence, and the position of the sentence in the document.

2. Clustering-based: This approach involves clustering similar sentences together and selecting one or more representative sentences from each cluster to form the summary. The clustering can be performed based on various similarity metrics, such as cosine similarity, Jaccard similarity, and Euclidean distance.

3. Machine learning-based: This approach involves training machine learning models, such as Support Vector Machines (SVMs), Random Forests, and Neural Networks, to classify sentences as either important or unimportant. The selected important sentences are then used to generate the summary.

Despite its advantages, extractive summarization also has some limitations. One of the primary limitations is that it can result in a summary that may not be well-structured and may not convey the complete meaning of the original text. Additionally, it may not be able to generate a summary that includes novel information or that provides a comprehensive overview of the document.

To address these limitations, researchers have developed another approach to text summarization known as abstractive summarization. Unlike extractive summarization, abstractive summarization involves generating new sentences that capture the meaning of the original text. This approach has gained a lot of attention in recent years due to its ability to generate summaries that are more readable and that capture the essential meaning of the original text.

9.2 Abstractive Summarization

Abstractive summarization is a more advanced approach to summarization that involves generating a summary that is not a direct extraction of sentences from the original text, but rather a new sentence or set of sentences that convey the most important information in the document. This approach requires natural language generation techniques to create a summary that reads like it was written by a human, which can be challenging.

One common technique used in abstractive summarization is the use of neural networks, particularly deep learning models such as recurrent neural networks (RNNs) and transformers. These models are trained on large amounts of data to learn how to generate summaries that capture the most important information in the original text. The models typically use an encoder-decoder architecture, where the encoder encodes the input text into a fixed-length vector representation and the decoder generates the summary based on this representation.

Another approach to abstractive summarization involves semantic analysis, which involves analyzing the meaning of the text to identify the most important concepts and ideas. This can be done using techniques such as topic modeling, named entity recognition, and sentiment analysis. Machine learning algorithms can then be used to generate a summary that captures these key concepts and ideas.

While abstractive summarization can produce more readable and concise summaries than extractive summarization, it is also a more challenging task that requires more advanced techniques and models. As a result, abstractive summarization is still an active area of research in the field of natural language processing.

9.3 Evaluation Metrics for Text Summarization

The effectiveness of text summarization algorithms is typically evaluated using metrics that compare the generated summary with a human-generated reference summary. Some commonly used evaluation metrics for text summarization include:

1. ROUGE: Recall-Oriented Understudy for Gisting Evaluation (ROUGE) is a set of metrics that compares the generated summary with one or more reference summaries. ROUGE measures the overlap between the generated summary and the reference summaries based on n-gram matching and sentence level similarity.

2. BLEU: The Bilingual Evaluation Understudy (BLEU) is a metric that compares the generated summary with one or more reference summaries based on n-gram matching. BLEU measures the precision of the generated summary in terms of the number of overlapping n-grams with the reference summary.

3. Pyramid: Pyramid is a metric that evaluates the quality of the generated summary based on its ability to capture the most important information in the original text. Pyramid uses a set of weighted criteria, such as content selection, clarity, and coherence, to evaluate the generated summary.

4. F-measure: The F-measure is a metric that combines precision and recall to evaluate the quality of the generated summary. The F-measure is the harmonic mean of precision and recall and provides a single score that indicates the effectiveness of the summarization algorithm.

9.4 Summary of the chapter

Text summarization is an important task in natural language processing, and there are two main approaches: extractive and abstractive summarization. Extractive summarization involves selecting important sentences or phrases from the original text, while abstractive summarization involves generating a summary that is not necessarily a subset of the original text. Evaluation metrics for text summarization include ROUGE, BLEU, Pyramid, and F-measure, which measure the effectiveness of the summarization algorithms in terms of their ability to capture important information from the original text.

Chapter 10: Applications of NLP

Introduction

Natural Language Processing (NLP) is a subfield of Artificial Intelligence that focuses on the interaction between humans and computers using natural language. NLP has a wide range of applications that can improve the way we communicate with technology. In this chapter, we will discuss some of the most common applications of NLP.

10.1 Chatbots and Conversational Agents

Chatbots and conversational agents are AI-powered computer programs designed to simulate human conversation using natural language processing techniques. They are designed to interact with users through chat or voice-based interfaces and can be integrated with messaging platforms, websites, mobile applications, and voice assistants.

One of the main applications of chatbots and conversational agents is in customer service. They can provide instant responses to customer queries, complaints, and requests, without the need for human intervention. This can help improve customer satisfaction and reduce wait times for support. Additionally, chatbots can handle routine tasks, such as account inquiries, password resets, and order tracking, allowing human agents to focus on more complex issues.

Personal assistants, such as Apple's Siri, Amazon's Alexa, and Google Assistant, are also examples of chatbots and conversational agents. These virtual assistants can perform a wide range of tasks, from setting reminders and scheduling appointments to playing music and controlling smart home devices. They use natural language processing techniques to understand user queries and respond appropriately. We will discuss this further in Chapter 10.6.

Entertainment is another area where chatbots and conversational agents are gaining popularity. Many chatbots are designed to provide entertainment to users, such as by telling jokes, playing games, or generating random facts. They can also be used for educational purposes, such as language learning or trivia quizzes.

10.2 Question Answering Systems

Question Answering Systems (QAS) are a type of NLP application that allows users to pose natural language questions and receive answers in the same format. These systems are designed to understand the meaning of a question and retrieve relevant information from a database or the web, making them useful for a variety of applications in different fields.

QAS can be used in education, where they can provide students with immediate feedback on their questions and help them learn new concepts. For example, a QAS designed for biology students can help answer questions about the human body, such as "What is the function of the pancreas?" or "What is the structure of a red blood cell?"

In healthcare, QAS can be used to provide patients with answers to common medical questions, such as "What are the symptoms of a heart attack?" or "What is the recommended treatment for diabetes?"

In customer service, QAS can help automate routine tasks and reduce the workload of customer support agents. For example, a QAS can be used to answer frequently asked questions about a product or service, such as "What are the hours of operation?" or "How do I reset my password?"

QAS can also be used in the legal field, where they can help lawyers and legal researchers find relevant information quickly and efficiently. For example, a QAS designed for legal professionals can help answer questions about specific laws or legal cases, such as "What is the statute of limitations for a personal injury claim?" or "What was the outcome of the landmark Supreme Court case Brown v. Board of Education?"

10.3 Machine Translation

Machine Translation (MT) is a field of natural language processing (NLP) that deals with the automatic translation of text from one language to another. It has become an essential tool for businesses, governments, and individuals to communicate and collaborate across different languages and cultures.

MT systems use various approaches to translate text, including rule-based, statistical, and neural machine translation. Rule-based MT systems use handcrafted rules and dictionaries to translate text from one language to another. Statistical machine translation systems, on the other hand, use statistical models that learn from large amounts of bilingual text to generate translations. These models use probabilistic algorithms to determine the best translation for a given input sentence. Neural machine translation systems use artificial neural networks to learn the patterns and structures of language and generate translations. They are considered the most advanced and accurate approach to MT.

The applications of MT are numerous, ranging from website localization and content translation to international business communication and diplomacy. MT is used by multinational corporations to translate marketing materials, technical documentation, and customer support content. Governments use MT to translate legal and official documents, as well as to improve communication with foreign partners. MT is also used by individuals for personal communication, such as emails and social media messages, and for translating news articles, books, and other materials.

Despite its benefits, MT has some limitations. Translation quality can vary depending on the complexity of the source text and the language pair being translated. MT systems may struggle with idiomatic expressions, cultural references, and nuances of language that require human interpretation. Therefore, it is important to evaluate the quality of translations generated by MT systems to ensure accuracy and avoid misunderstandings.

10.4 Text-to-Speech Systems

Text-to-Speech (TTS) systems are computer programs that convert written text into spoken language. TTS technology has advanced significantly in recent years, with the development of neural network-based systems that generate natural-sounding speech. TTS systems are used in a variety of applications, including accessibility tools for the visually impaired, language learning software, and entertainment.

One of the main benefits of TTS systems is their ability to make written content accessible to those who are visually impaired. TTS technology can be used to read out books, news articles, and other written materials, allowing visually impaired individuals to access the same content as sighted individuals. TTS systems can also be used to provide real-time feedback to users with visual impairments, such as describing the content of an image or providing navigation instructions.

TTS systems are also used in language learning software, where they can help students improve their pronunciation and listening skills. By hearing words and phrases pronounced correctly, students can learn to speak a language more fluently and accurately. TTS systems can also be used to provide feedback on pronunciation, allowing students to identify and correct errors in their pronunciation.

In the entertainment industry, TTS systems are used to create voiceovers for movies, TV shows, and video games. TTS technology can generate high-quality, natural-sounding speech that can be used to create compelling voiceovers for characters and narrators. TTS systems are also used in virtual assistants, where they can provide users with personalized responses and interact with users in a more natural and conversational manner.

10.5 Natural Language Interfaces for Search Engines

Natural Language Interfaces for Search Engines (NLISE) are designed to allow users to interact with search engines using natural language queries, rather than relying on a keyword-based search. These systems are becoming increasingly popular as they provide a more intuitive and user-friendly way to search for information. NLISE systems use natural language processing (NLP) techniques to understand the user's intent and generate relevant search results.

One of the benefits of NLISE is that it allows users to ask questions in their own words, without having to worry about using the right keywords or search terms. This can be particularly useful for non-experts who may not be familiar with the specific jargon or technical terminology associated with a particular topic. NLISE can also help users to find information more quickly and easily, as it can provide direct answers to specific questions, rather than requiring users to sift through a large number of search results.

NLISE systems can use various techniques to understand natural language queries, such as named entity recognition, semantic analysis, and machine learning algorithms. Named entity recognition involves identifying and categorizing entities mentioned in the user's query, such as people, organizations, and locations. Semantic analysis involves analyzing the meaning of the user's query and identifying the key concepts or topics that they are interested in. Machine learning algorithms can be used to improve the accuracy of NLISE systems over time, by learning from user interactions and feedback.

10.6 Virtual Assistants

Virtual Assistants (VAs) are NLP-based systems that use speech recognition and natural language processing (NLP) to understand and respond to user requests. They are designed to perform various tasks, such as setting reminders, scheduling appointments, and sending emails. VAs are also known as intelligent personal assistants or digital assistants, and they are becoming increasingly popular in both personal and professional settings.

VAs are programmed with the ability to recognize and understand natural language, allowing users to interact with them in a conversational manner. VAs can be accessed through mobile devices, smart speakers, and other digital devices. They can also be integrated with other applications, such as calendars, email clients, and messaging apps, to streamline various tasks and improve productivity.

One of the most well-known virtual assistants is Apple's Siri, which was introduced in 2011. Other popular VAs include Amazon's Alexa, Google Assistant, and Microsoft's Cortana. These VAs are capable of performing a wide range of tasks, including playing music, setting reminders, and answering questions. They can also be programmed to control smart home devices, such as thermostats, lights, and security systems.

Virtual assistants are increasingly being used in business settings as well, with companies using them to improve productivity and efficiency. For example, VAs can be used to schedule meetings, send reminders, and manage tasks for employees. They can also be used to provide customer support, allowing customers to interact with the company through natural language queries.

While virtual assistants have many benefits, they also raise concerns about privacy and security. VAs often collect user data to improve their performance, which raises concerns about the privacy of that data. In addition, there have been concerns about the security of virtual assistants, with reports of VAs being hacked and used to access sensitive information.

10.7 Sentiment Analysis for Social Media Monitoring

Sentiment Analysis (SA) is a technique used in natural language processing to identify the sentiment of a piece of text, such as a tweet or a product review. SA aims to determine whether the sentiment of the text is positive, negative, or neutral. This technique has become increasingly important in recent years due to the explosion of social media and online reviews.

SA can be used for various applications, such as brand monitoring, customer feedback analysis, and public opinion analysis. By analyzing social media content, businesses can gain insights into customer sentiment towards their products or services and use that information to improve their offerings. SA can also be used to monitor brand reputation and identify potential issues before they become major problems.

There are several approaches to SA, including rule-based systems, machine learning, and deep learning. Rule-based systems use a set of predefined rules to identify sentiment words and phrases and assign a sentiment score. Machine learning approaches use a labeled dataset to train a model to recognize sentiment in text. Deep learning approaches, such as neural networks, use multiple layers to learn features from the data and make predictions.

SA evaluation metrics include accuracy, precision, recall, and F1-score. Accuracy measures the overall correctness of the SA system's predictions, while precision measures the proportion of true positives among all positive predictions. Recall measures the proportion of true positives among all actual positive instances, and the F1-score is the harmonic mean of precision and recall.

10.8 Chatbots for Customer Service

Chatbots have revolutionized the customer service industry by providing quick and efficient support to customers. By using natural language processing techniques, chatbots can understand the user's query and provide relevant information or assistance. This can help reduce response time, increase customer satisfaction, and ultimately lead to higher sales and customer loyalty.

Chatbots can handle routine inquiries and tasks, such as order status, delivery information, and product information. This allows human agents to focus on more complex issues that require human intervention, such as resolving customer complaints or providing personalized support.

In addition to reducing response time, chatbots can also help businesses save costs. Since chatbots can provide 24/7 support, businesses can reduce their staffing costs by relying on chatbots to handle routine inquiries during non-business hours. This can also help businesses scale their support operations without having to hire additional human agents.

Moreover, chatbots can improve the overall customer experience by providing personalized and proactive support. By analyzing customer data, chatbots can anticipate customer needs and provide relevant information or recommendations. This can help businesses build stronger relationships with their customers and increase customer loyalty.

10.9 Speech Recognition

Speech Recognition (SR) is a technology that enables machines to recognize and interpret human speech. It involves converting spoken language into text, which can then be processed and analyzed by computers. The main goal of SR is to accurately transcribe spoken words into written text, while also taking into account factors such as pronunciation, accents, and background noise.

SR has a wide range of applications, including voice assistants, dictation software, and language learning tools. Voice assistants, such as Siri, Alexa, and Google Assistant, use SR to understand user commands and respond appropriately. Dictation software, such as Dragon NaturallySpeaking, allows users to dictate text instead of typing it. Language learning tools, such as Duolingo, use SR to help learners improve their pronunciation and speaking skills.

SR systems use various techniques to recognize and interpret spoken language. These include Hidden Markov Models (HMMs), neural networks, and statistical models. HMMs are a type of probabilistic model that can be used to model speech sounds and recognize patterns in speech. Neural networks are a type of machine learning model that can be used to learn complex patterns in speech data. Statistical models use probability theory to model speech and language, and are commonly used in speech recognition systems.

10.10 Summary of the chapter

NLP has become an essential technology in today's digital world, and its applications are widespread. From chatbots and conversational agents to machine translation and speech recognition, NLP is changing the way we communicate with technology. As the technology continues to evolve, we can expect to see even more applications of NLP in the future.

Chapter 11: Programming languages and toosl commonly used in NLP

Natural Language Processing (NLP) is a field of computer science and artificial intelligence that focuses on the interaction between human language and computers. In order to develop NLP applications, developers and researchers use programming languages and tools that are specifically designed for natural language processing tasks. In this chapter, we will explore some of the most popular programming languages and tools commonly used in NLP, including Python, NLTK, spaCy, Stanford CoreNLP, Gensim, TensorFlow, and PyTorch.

11.1 Python

Python is a general-purpose programming language that has gained widespread adoption in the NLP community due to its robust ecosystem of libraries and tools. Python's syntax is simple and easy to read, making it an excellent language for rapid prototyping and experimentation.

Python's popularity in the NLP community is largely due to its extensive range of libraries and tools specifically designed for natural language processing tasks. The Natural Language Toolkit (NLTK) is a comprehensive Python library for NLP that provides a suite of tools and resources for text processing and analysis. NLTK includes a wide range of modules for tokenization, stemming, tagging, parsing, and classification, as well as access to large corpora and lexicons. NLTK is widely used in academic and research environments due to its ease of use and extensive documentation.

spaCy is another popular Python library for NLP that focuses on high-performance text processing and analysis. It is known for its speed and efficiency, as well as its ability to handle large-scale text processing tasks. spaCy includes modules for tokenization, part-of-speech tagging, dependency parsing, and named entity recognition, among others. spaCy is used in industry and research settings for various NLP applications, such as information extraction, sentiment analysis, and chatbots.

Python's popularity in NLP has also been driven by the availability of deep learning frameworks such as TensorFlow and PyTorch. These frameworks provide efficient tools for training and deploying neural network models, which have become increasingly popular in NLP applications such as language translation, sentiment analysis, and text generation.

Python's versatility extends beyond NLP, as it can be used for a wide range of other applications such as web development, data analysis, and scientific computing. Due to its ease of use, large developer community, and vast library of tools, Python is likely to remain a popular choice for NLP developers for years to come.

11.2 Stanford CoreNLP

Stanford CoreNLP is a comprehensive suite of NLP tools that has been widely adopted in both academic and industry settings for its accuracy and robustness. The suite includes a wide range of modules that cover many aspects of NLP, such as tokenization, part-of-speech tagging, parsing, named entity recognition, sentiment analysis, and coreference resolution.

One of the main advantages of Stanford CoreNLP is its accuracy. It is based on state-of-the-art algorithms and models developed by the Stanford Natural Language Processing Group, which has a long history of NLP research and expertise. This accuracy has been demonstrated in various benchmark datasets and challenges, where Stanford CoreNLP consistently ranks among the top performers.

Another advantage of Stanford CoreNLP is its ease of use. It provides a user-friendly interface that allows developers to easily access and use the different modules. The suite can be accessed through a web service or a command-line interface, making it easy to integrate into existing applications and workflows.

Furthermore, Stanford CoreNLP is open-source, which means that the source code is available for anyone to use, modify, and distribute. This has led to a large and active community of developers and researchers who have contributed to the suite's development and improvement over the years.

11.3 Gensim

Gensim is a powerful Python library for natural language processing that provides a range of tools and algorithms for topic modeling and semantic analysis. It is designed to be efficient, scalable, and easy to use, making it a popular choice for researchers and practitioners in the field of NLP.

One of the main features of Gensim is its support for topic modeling, which is the process of identifying topics or themes in a collection of documents.

Gensim provides several algorithms for topic modeling, including Latent Dirichlet Allocation (LDA), which is one of the most widely used algorithms in the field. Gensim also provides tools for evaluating the quality of topic models, such as coherence measures and visualization tools.

Another important feature of Gensim is its support for word embedding, which is the process of representing words as vectors in a high-dimensional space. Gensim provides several algorithms for word embedding, including Word2Vec and GloVe. These algorithms are widely used in applications such as sentiment analysis, document classification, and information retrieval.

Gensim also provides tools for similarity detection, such as cosine similarity and Jaccard similarity, which can be used to compare documents or identify similar words and phrases. In addition, Gensim includes modules for document indexing and retrieval, which can be used to build search engines and recommendation systems.

11.4 TensorFlow

TensorFlow is an end-to-end open-source platform for building and deploying machine learning models developed by the Google Brain team. It provides a comprehensive set of tools and libraries for building and training machine learning models across multiple domains, including natural language processing.

TensorFlow has become popular in the NLP community due to its flexibility, scalability, and high performance. It supports a wide range of neural network architectures, including convolutional neural networks (CNNs), recurrent neural networks (RNNs), long short-term memory (LSTM) networks, and transformers. These architectures can be used for various NLP tasks, such as sentiment analysis, text classification, machine translation, and language modeling.

TensorFlow also offers a wide range of pre-trained models and datasets that can be easily integrated into NLP pipelines. For example, the Universal Sentence Encoder is a pre-trained model that can be used for sentence-level embeddings, allowing for faster and more accurate processing of large text datasets.

TensorFlow is known for its ease of use and simplicity. Its high-level APIs, such as Keras, provide an intuitive interface for building and training machine learning models, allowing developers to focus on their application logic rather than the low-level details of the model architecture.

TensorFlow has a vibrant community of developers and researchers who contribute to its development and improvement. This community provides extensive documentation, tutorials, and support for users of all levels.

11.5 PyTorch

PyTorch is an open-source machine learning framework developed by Facebook's AI Research (FAIR) team, released in 2016. It is a popular choice among researchers and practitioners in the NLP field due to its ease of use and flexibility. PyTorch provides a dynamic computational graph that allows for more efficient computation of complex models compared to static computational graphs used by other frameworks such as TensorFlow.

One of the key features of PyTorch is its support for neural network building and training. PyTorch provides a comprehensive set of tools for building neural networks of different architectures, including recurrent neural networks (RNNs), convolutional neural networks (CNNs), and transformers, which are particularly useful for NLP tasks such as language modeling, machine translation, and sentiment analysis.

PyTorch provides several high-level modules such as torch.nn and torch.optim that allow developers to build and train complex neural network models with ease. The torch.nn module provides a set of pre-defined building blocks such as layers, activation functions, and loss functions that can be combined to create complex neural networks. The torch.optim module provides various optimization algorithms such as Stochastic Gradient Descent (SGD), Adam, and Adagrad, which can be used to optimize the network parameters during training.

Another advantage of PyTorch is its support for GPU acceleration, which allows for faster training of models. PyTorch also provides a dynamic computation graph, which means that the graph is built on the fly during the execution of the program, allowing for more flexibility in model development.

In addition to NLP, PyTorch is also used for other machine learning tasks such as computer vision and speech recognition. PyTorch has a growing community of developers and users who contribute to the development of the framework and its ecosystem of libraries and tools.

11.6 Summary of the chapter

Programming languages and tools are essential for developing NLP applications that can process and analyze human language. Python, NLTK, spaCy, Stanford CoreNLP, Gensim, TensorFlow, and PyTorch are some of the most commonly used programming languages and tools in the field of NLP. Python, with its simplicity and ease of use, has emerged as a popular choice for developing NLP applications. Its rich collection of libraries, such as NLTK, spaCy, and Gensim, makes it easier to perform various NLP tasks.

NLP is a rapidly growing field, and programming languages and tools play a critical role in its development. Python and its associated libraries are widely used in the industry and academia due to their ease of use, extensive documentation, and active development communities. As NLP continues to advance, we can expect to see new programming languages and tools emerge, providing developers with even more powerful tools for building intelligent language-based applications.

Chapter 12: Techniques for handling large-scale NLP problems

As NLP problems continue to grow in complexity and scale, handling large amounts of data becomes a challenge. To address this challenge, various techniques have been developed to enable efficient processing of large-scale NLP problems. In this chapter, we will discuss some of the most common techniques used for handling large-scale NLP problems: distributed computing, parallel processing, and cloud computing.

12.1 Distributed Computing

Distributed computing is a technique that involves splitting a large task into smaller sub-tasks and assigning each sub-task to a separate computer or server. The computers work in parallel to solve the sub-tasks, and the results are combined to produce the final output. Distributed computing enables processing of large volumes of data in a shorter time compared to a single computer.

One of the most popular distributed computing frameworks for NLP is Apache Hadoop. Hadoop is an open-source framework that allows processing of large-scale datasets by breaking them into smaller parts and distributing them across a cluster of computers. Hadoop includes tools like MapReduce, which can process large volumes of data in parallel, and HDFS, a distributed file system for storing and managing large datasets.

12.2 Parallel Processing

Parallel processing is another technique used for handling large-scale NLP problems. In parallel processing, a large task is broken down into smaller tasks that can be processed simultaneously on different cores of the same computer. This technique can speed up the processing time and reduce the overall computational cost.

One popular tool for parallel processing in NLP is Apache Spark. Spark is an open-source framework that can handle large-scale data processing across a distributed cluster. Spark can be used for various NLP tasks, such as text classification, natural language understanding, and sentiment analysis.

12.3 Cloud Computing

Cloud computing is a technique that enables access to computing resources and storage over the internet. Cloud computing allows users to rent computing resources, such as servers and storage, on-demand and pay only for what they use. This makes it an ideal solution for handling large-scale NLP problems as users can scale their resources up or down based on their needs.

One popular cloud computing service used for NLP is Amazon Web Services (AWS). AWS offers various services, such as Amazon EC2 (Elastic Compute Cloud) for computing resources, Amazon S3 (Simple Storage Service) for data storage, and Amazon EMR (Elastic MapReduce) for distributed data processing.

12.4 Summary of the chapter

As NLP problems become increasingly complex and large in scale, handling them efficiently becomes a challenge. However, distributed computing, parallel processing, and cloud computing are powerful techniques that enable efficient processing of large-scale NLP problems. These techniques can help NLP researchers and practitioners to process large amounts of data quickly and cost-effectively, thereby enabling the development of more sophisticated and accurate NLP models and applications.

Chapter 13: Best practices for data preparation and model selection

Data preparation and model selection are crucial components in developing effective NLP models. In this chapter, we will discuss some of the best practices for data preparation and model selection, including data sampling, feature engineering, hyperparameter tuning, and cross-validation.

13.1 Data Sampling:

Data sampling is an essential step in NLP data preparation, especially when working with large datasets. It involves selecting a subset of data from the original dataset that can be used for training and testing machine learning models. The choice of data sample is crucial because it can affect the accuracy of the model. Therefore, it is essential to select a representative subset of the data that accurately reflects the characteristics of the larger dataset.

One commonly used technique for data sampling in NLP is stratified sampling. In this approach, the dataset is divided into several strata based on the classes or labels of the data. Then, a random sample is selected from each stratum based on the proportion of data in that stratum to the total dataset. This ensures that the sample is representative of the original dataset's class distribution, which is important in tasks such as sentiment analysis or classification.

Another approach to data sampling is random sampling, where a random subset of the data is selected without considering the class distribution. Random sampling is more straightforward than stratified sampling but may not provide a representative sample of the dataset. In some cases, random sampling may be appropriate if the dataset is well balanced, and the sample size is large enough to capture the dataset's variability.

It is essential to evaluate the performance of the machine learning model on the sample data. The evaluation metrics, such as precision, recall, and F1 score, can provide insights into the model's performance on the sample data. However, it is important to note that the evaluation on the sample data may not always reflect the model's performance on the entire dataset.

13.2 Feature Engineering

Feature engineering is the process of selecting and transforming the raw data into a set of features that are more useful for the model. In NLP, feature engineering involves transforming text data into a set of numerical features that can be used as input to the model.

Bag-of-words is a popular feature engineering technique in NLP, where each document or sentence is represented as a bag of its constituent words. The order of the words is not taken into account, and the resulting feature matrix is typically large and sparse. One variation of bag-of-words is the n-gram model, where sequences of n consecutive words are used as features instead of individual words. This approach can capture some of the context and syntax of the text, but can also lead to overfitting when n is too large.

Another feature engineering technique is term frequency-inverse document frequency (tf-idf), which is used to weigh the importance of each word in a document or corpus. The tf-idf weight is calculated as the product of the term frequency (tf) and the inverse document frequency (idf). The term frequency measures how often a term appears in a document, while the inverse document frequency measures how rare a term is across the entire corpus. The resulting tf-idf matrix is typically smaller and sparser than the bag-of-words matrix, and can capture the relative importance of different words in the text.

Word embeddings are a more recent technique for feature engineering in NLP, where each word is represented as a dense vector in a high-dimensional space. Word embeddings are learned from a large corpus using neural network models such as word2vec, GloVe, or fastText. The resulting word embeddings capture the semantic and syntactic relationships between words, and can be used as input to various NLP models such as neural networks or support vector machines (SVMs).

Finally, character n-grams are another feature engineering technique that can be used to capture the morphology and spelling of words. Instead of using individual words or n-grams of words, character n-grams are sequences of n consecutive characters, such as trigrams or four-grams. These features can capture the morphological variations of words and can be useful for tasks such as authorship attribution or text classification.

13.3 Hyperparameter Tuning

Hyperparameters are parameters that are set before the training of the model and affect the performance of the model. Hyperparameter tuning involves selecting the best set of hyperparameters that result in the highest performance of the model. Common hyperparameters in NLP models include the learning rate, number of layers, batch size, and regularization parameters. A common technique for hyperparameter tuning is grid search, where a range of values for each hyperparameter is tested to determine the best combination.

Another common technique for hyperparameter tuning is random search, where a set of hyperparameters is randomly sampled from a distribution. This technique can be more efficient than grid search, as it does not require testing every possible combination of hyperparameters. Additionally, Bayesian optimization is another approach to hyperparameter tuning, where a probabilistic model is used to predict the performance of different hyperparameter configurations. This approach can be more efficient than grid search and random search, as it can use past evaluations to guide the search and explore promising regions of the hyperparameter space.

It is important to note that hyperparameter tuning can be a time-consuming process, especially for large NLP models. It is recommended to use parallel processing techniques to speed up the process, such as running multiple training jobs in parallel or using distributed computing frameworks like Apache Spark. Additionally, it is crucial to use a validation set to evaluate the performance of the model during hyperparameter tuning, as using the test set can lead to overfitting and biased results.

Lastly, it is essential to record the hyperparameters used for each experiment to facilitate reproducibility and to enable comparison of the results between different experiments. This practice can help identify the best hyperparameters for a given NLP problem and provide insights for future research.

13.4 Cross-Validation

Cross-validation is an important technique for ensuring that NLP models are not overfitting the data and are generalizing well to new data. It involves splitting the data into multiple folds and training the model on each fold while evaluating its performance on the remaining folds. This helps to obtain a more accurate estimate of the model's performance than simply evaluating it on a single validation set.

There are several types of cross-validation techniques, including k-fold cross-validation, stratified k-fold cross-validation, leave-one-out cross-validation, and holdout cross-validation. In k-fold cross-validation, the data is divided into k equal folds, and the model is trained and validated k times, with each fold being used once for validation and the remaining k-1 folds being used for training. Stratified k-fold cross-validation is similar, but it ensures that each fold contains approximately the same proportion of each class.

Leave-one-out cross-validation is a special case of k-fold cross-validation, where k is equal to the number of samples in the dataset. This is computationally expensive, but can provide a more accurate estimate of the model's performance. Holdout cross-validation involves splitting the data into a training set and a validation set, and training the model on the training set while evaluating its performance on the validation set.

Cross-validation is a useful technique for selecting the best model and hyperparameters for an NLP task. By comparing the performance of different models and hyperparameters across multiple folds, it is possible to obtain a more accurate estimate of the model's performance on new data. It is important to note, however, that cross-validation can be computationally expensive, particularly for large datasets or complex models. In some cases, a simpler validation strategy, such as a single validation set, may be sufficient.

13.5 Summary of the chapter

Data preparation and model selection are essential components of developing effective NLP models. Data sampling, feature engineering, hyperparameter tuning, and cross-validation are some of the best practices for ensuring the performance and generalizability of NLP models.

Chapter 14: Ethical considerations in NLP

Introduction: Natural Language Processing (NLP) has grown exponentially in recent years, and it is being used in various applications such as chatbots, sentiment analysis, speech recognition, and language translation. However, NLP also raises ethical considerations that need to be addressed. These considerations include bias, privacy, and security. This chapter will explore each of these topics in-depth and provide insights into how to address them.

14.1 Bias

Bias in NLP refers to the systematic and unfair treatment of certain groups of people based on their characteristics such as gender, race, religion, and sexual orientation. Bias in NLP can manifest in different ways, such as biased training data, biased algorithms, and biased output. Biased training data can lead to biased models, and biased models can lead to biased output, which can have serious implications.

To address bias in NLP, it is important to start with unbiased training data. This can be achieved by ensuring that the training data is representative of the population and includes data from diverse groups. It is also essential to ensure that the data is labeled correctly and does not contain any discriminatory or offensive content.

Another approach to addressing bias in NLP is to use algorithms that are designed to be fair and unbiased. These algorithms are typically trained on data that has been preprocessed to remove any biases. They are also designed to avoid learning from correlations between protected attributes such as gender and occupation.

14.2 Privacy

Privacy in NLP refers to the protection of personal information that is collected, processed, and analyzed during NLP tasks. NLP applications can collect sensitive information such as health data, financial information, and personal conversations. It is essential to ensure that this information is protected and used only for the intended purpose.

To address privacy concerns in NLP, it is important to have clear guidelines and policies for the collection, storage, and use of personal data. These guidelines should ensure that personal data is collected only with the consent of the individual and is used only for the intended purpose. It is also essential to ensure that personal data is stored securely and is not accessible to unauthorized individuals.

Another approach to addressing privacy concerns in NLP is to use techniques such as differential privacy. Differential privacy is a technique for anonymizing data by adding noise to the data in such a way that it does not affect the accuracy of the analysis but makes it difficult to identify individual data points.

14.3 Security

Security in NLP refers to the protection of NLP systems from malicious attacks such as hacking, data breaches, and malware. NLP systems can be vulnerable to attacks because they often use large amounts of data, and the algorithms used in these systems can be complex.

To address security concerns in NLP, it is important to ensure that the NLP system is designed with security in mind. This can be achieved by implementing security measures such as access controls, data encryption, and secure communication protocols. It is also essential to ensure that the NLP system is regularly monitored for potential security threats and vulnerabilities.

Another approach to addressing security concerns in NLP is to use techniques such as adversarial training. Adversarial training involves training the NLP system on data that has been intentionally modified to test the system's ability to detect and defend against attacks.

14.4 Summary of the chapter

As NLP becomes more prevalent in various applications, it is essential to consider the ethical implications of this technology. Bias, privacy, and security are three critical areas that need to be addressed to ensure that NLP is used ethically and responsibly. By addressing these concerns, we can ensure that NLP technology is used for the benefit of all individuals and does not harm or discriminate against any group.

Chapter 15: NLP research and development

With the advent of machine learning and deep learning, NLP has seen a surge in research and development. In this chapter, we will discuss the current trends in NLP research, academic conferences, research groups, and how to get involved in the NLP community.

15.1 Current research trends

NLP research is an active field that involves a wide range of topics, including text classification, sentiment analysis, machine translation, question-answering, and more. Some current trends in NLP research include:

1. Deep Learning: Deep learning has revolutionized NLP research by enabling the creation of models that can learn from large amounts of data. Deep learning models, such as convolutional neural networks (CNNs) and recurrent neural networks (RNNs), have shown significant improvements in various NLP tasks.

2. Language Models: Language models are algorithms that can generate text based on a given context. Recent advances in language models have resulted in the development of models like GPT-3, which can generate human-like text.

3. Multimodal NLP: Multimodal NLP involves the analysis of text along with other modalities, such as images and audio. This field has seen significant advancements in recent years, with the development of

models that can understand and generate natural language from multimodal inputs.

15.2 Academic conferences

Academic conferences are an excellent way to keep up with the latest developments in NLP research. Some of the top conferences in the field include:

1. ACL: The Association for Computational Linguistics hosts an annual conference that covers all aspects of NLP research.

2. EMNLP: The Conference on Empirical Methods in Natural Language Processing focuses on the practical aspects of NLP research, including machine translation, information retrieval, and more.

3. NAACL: The North American Chapter of the Association for Computational Linguistics hosts an annual conference that covers all aspects of NLP research.

15.3 Research groups

There are several research groups and labs around the world that are dedicated to NLP research. Some of the most prominent research groups include:

1. Google Brain: Google Brain is a research group at Google that focuses on machine learning and AI research, including NLP.

2. Facebook AI Research (FAIR): FAIR is a research group at Facebook that focuses on AI research, including NLP.

3. Allen Institute for Artificial Intelligence (AI2): AI2 is a research institute that focuses on AI research, including NLP.

15.4 How to get involved in the NLP community

Getting involved in the NLP community is a great way to learn more about the field and connect with other researchers. Some ways to get involved include:

1. Attend academic conferences: Attending academic conferences is an excellent way to learn about the latest research in the field and connect with other researchers.

2. Join online communities: There are several online communities, such as Reddit's NLP community and the NLP group on LinkedIn, where researchers can discuss NLP topics and share their work.

3. Participate in NLP challenges: NLP challenges, such as those hosted on Kaggle, are an excellent way to test your skills and learn from other researchers.

15.5 Summary of the chapter

NLP research is a rapidly growing field that involves the use of computer algorithms to analyze and understand human language. With the advent of machine learning and deep learning, NLP has seen a surge in research and development. Attending academic conferences, joining online communities, and participating in NLP challenges are all great ways to get involved in the NLP community and stay up-to-date with the latest developments in the field.

Chapter 16: Resources for NLP

Introduction

In recent years, there has been a tremendous growth in the amount of data available for NLP tasks. To facilitate this growth, there are several resources available for researchers and practitioners in the field. In this chapter, we will discuss some of the most important resources for NLP, including pre-trained models, word embeddings, lexicons, and corpora.

16.1 Pre-Trained Models

Pre-trained models are becoming increasingly popular in NLP due to their ability to save time and resources in the model development process. These models are trained on massive datasets, often using advanced techniques such as deep learning, to learn patterns and relationships in language data. The resulting model can then be fine-tuned or adapted for a specific task or domain with smaller datasets, which can lead to improved performance and reduced development time.

BERT, or Bidirectional Encoder Representations from Transformers, is one of the most popular pre-trained models for NLP. It is a deep learning model that is trained on a large corpus of text, such as Wikipedia and the BookCorpus, using an unsupervised learning approach. BERT has been fine-tuned for a wide range of NLP tasks, including question answering, sentiment analysis, and language translation.

GPT, or Generative Pre-trained Transformer, is another pre-trained model that is widely used in NLP research and applications. It is a language model that has been trained on a large corpus of text using an unsupervised learning approach. GPT can be fine-tuned for a variety of NLP tasks, such as text generation, summarization, and question answering.

ELMo, or Embeddings from Language Models, is a deep contextualized word embedding model that has been pre-trained on a large corpus of text using a bi-directional LSTM. It can generate word embeddings that capture the meaning of a word based on its context within a sentence, which can be useful for downstream NLP tasks such as sentiment analysis and named entity recognition.

In addition to these popular pre-trained models, there are many others available for various NLP tasks and languages. Many of these models are available for download and use through open-source repositories such as Hugging Face's Transformers library and the AllenNLP library.

One of the benefits of pre-trained models is that they can reduce the need for large amounts of labeled data, which can be expensive and time-consuming to collect. However, it is important to note that pre-trained models can still contain biases and limitations, which can impact their performance on specific tasks or domains. Therefore, it is important to evaluate and fine-tune pre-trained models for specific use cases and ensure that they are appropriate for the intended application.

16.2 Word Embeddings

Word embeddings are a type of representation of words as vectors, where each vector represents the meaning of the corresponding word. These vectors are generated using unsupervised machine learning techniques that analyze the co-occurrence patterns of words in large text corpora. Word embeddings capture the semantic meaning of words by representing them as points in a high-dimensional space, where the distance between two vectors indicates the degree of similarity between the corresponding words.

There are many benefits to using word embeddings in NLP. One of the most significant benefits is that they can reduce the dimensionality of the input data, making it easier and faster for models to process. Additionally, word embeddings can capture the context and meaning of words, which is essential for many NLP tasks.

One of the earliest and most popular word embedding models is Word2Vec, developed by Tomas Mikolov and colleagues at Google. Word2Vec uses a shallow neural network to predict the context of each word in a large text corpus. The output of this network is a set of vectors that represent each word in the corpus.

Another popular word embedding model is GloVe (Global Vectors for Word Representation), developed by researchers at Stanford University. GloVe uses a matrix factorization approach to generate word embeddings based on the co-occurrence statistics of words in a large corpus.

FastText is a more recent word embedding model developed by Facebook. Like Word2Vec, it uses a neural network to generate word embeddings, but it also incorporates subword information to handle rare words and misspellings.

Word embeddings are available in many pre-trained models, which can be used as a starting point for developing more advanced models. These pre-trained models are often trained on large corpora of text and can be fine-tuned on smaller datasets for specific NLP tasks. Additionally, word embeddings can be customized to specific domains by training them on domain-specific corpora.

16.3 Lexicons

To expand on the topic of lexicons in NLP, it is important to note that they are not limited to sentiment analysis but can also be used in other tasks such as named entity recognition and machine translation. They can also be used for tasks that require domain-specific knowledge, such as medical NLP, where medical lexicons can be used to extract information from medical records.

One of the challenges with using lexicons is their coverage and accuracy. Lexicons may not contain all the words in a given language, and the meanings of words can vary depending on the context in which they are used. Therefore, it is important to choose a lexicon that is appropriate for the task at hand and to evaluate its performance on a test set.

In addition to pre-built lexicons, domain-specific lexicons can be created by domain experts to capture domain-specific knowledge. These lexicons can be used to improve the performance of NLP models in the specific domain.

Furthermore, lexicons can also be used to build knowledge graphs, which are a collection of concepts and their relationships that can be used for various NLP tasks. Knowledge graphs are used in tasks such as question answering and information retrieval, where the goal is to extract information from unstructured text and provide a structured representation of the information.

16.4 Corpora

Corpora are a critical resource for natural language processing (NLP) research and development. They are collections of texts that have been curated and annotated for use in various NLP tasks. Corpora can range from relatively small collections of texts to massive datasets with millions of documents.

One of the most well-known corpora is the Penn Treebank, which is a collection of parsed and annotated text from sources such as the Wall Street Journal. This corpus is widely used for training and evaluating models for tasks such as part-of-speech tagging and parsing.

Another popular corpus is the Brown Corpus, which is a collection of text from various genres, including fiction, news, and academic writing. The Brown Corpus is often used for research on language variation and style.

In addition to these general-purpose corpora, there are also specialized corpora that are tailored to specific NLP tasks. For example, the CoNLL shared tasks have produced annotated corpora for tasks such as named entity recognition and semantic role labeling.

The availability of large, annotated corpora has been a key factor in the recent advances in NLP. These corpora enable researchers and developers to train and evaluate models on realistic data, which can improve the accuracy and generalizability of the models.

One challenge with corpora is that they may contain biased or sensitive content. For example, some corpora may contain offensive language or stereotypes that can propagate through the models trained on them. Therefore, it is essential to carefully curate and evaluate the content of corpora to ensure that they are ethical and fair.

16. 5 Summary of the chapter

NLP resources play a critical role in the development and advancement of NLP techniques and applications. Pre-trained models, word embeddings, lexicons, and corpora are just a few examples of the many resources that are available for researchers and practitioners in the field. By leveraging these resources, we can accelerate the pace of research and development in NLP, leading to new and innovative applications of this exciting field.

Chapter 17: Conclusion

industries. As technology continues to advance, NLP is expected to become even more important in the coming years. However, there are also challenges that need to be addressed, such as bias, privacy, and security.

One of the future trends in NLP is the development of more advanced models that can perform multiple NLP tasks simultaneously. These models, known as multi-task models, have the potential to significantly improve the performance of NLP systems.

Another trend is the development of NLP models that can understand and generate human-like language. This involves improving the models' ability to understand nuances, context, and emotions in language.

There is also a growing interest in applying NLP techniques to other areas, such as healthcare, finance, and legal industries. NLP can be used to analyze medical records, financial documents, and legal contracts, among other applications.

However, there are also challenges that need to be addressed in the field. One of the biggest challenges is bias in NLP systems, which can result in unfair and discriminatory outcomes. It is important for researchers and practitioners to develop methods to mitigate bias in NLP systems.

Privacy and security are also major concerns, especially as NLP is applied to sensitive data such as personal information and financial records. It is important to ensure that NLP systems are designed with privacy and security in mind.

In conclusion, NLP is a rapidly growing field with numerous applications and challenges. As technology continues to advance, NLP has the potential to revolutionize various industries and improve the way we communicate and interact with machines. However, it is important for researchers and practitioners to be mindful of the ethical implications of NLP and work towards creating systems that are fair, unbiased, and secure.

Chapter 18: References and further reading

1. "Speech and Language Processing" by Daniel Jurafsky and James H. Martin

2. "Natural Language Processing with Python" by Steven Bird, Ewan Klein, and Edward Loper

3. "Foundations of Statistical Natural Language Processing" by Christopher D. Manning and Hinrich Schütze

4. "Deep Learning for Natural Language Processing" by Palash Goyal, Sumit Pandey, and Karan Jain

5. "The Handbook of Computational Linguistics and Natural Language Processing" edited by Alexander Clark, Chris Fox, and Shalom Lappin

6. "Recent Advances in Natural Language Processing" edited by Ruslan Mitkov "The Unreasonable Effectiveness of Recurrent Neural Networks" by Andrej Karpathy